MAKE
THE
CEO
FIX IT

ISBN: 1-4392-0209-5
ISBN-13: 9781439202098

Visit www.booksurge.com to order additional copies.

MAKE
THE
CEO
FIX IT

Capturing Executive Attention Through Email

CHRIS MIELKE

*Dedicated to my loving wife and everyone
who has ever needed a hand in solving problems.*

Table of Contents

Preface

This book was born over a lunch conversation with a friend. He told me about the problems he was having getting a rebate check for a pair of cell phones he bought. He had called customer service, had spoken with several customer service managers and wasn't having any luck. They either could not find his information for the rebate (even though they billed him every month) or he was given excuses why it wasn't coming. He was ready to give up and just chalk up the rebate as a loss.

I waited for him to finish and then commented, "Why don't you email the CEO and the board of directors and tell them your problem?"

He looked back at me with a bewildered look and exclaimed, "Why? They won't listen. They already have my money."

I described to him the strategy I use when I encounter roadblocks with customer service and I know that I am not being treated fairly.

He listened intently and then said dubiously, "That's it? And they will listen?"

I couldn't make any guarantees, but he left to follow my directions.

The following day he came by my desk and thanked me. A vice president of the company was taking steps to send him his rebate within a week. The company was also going to issue him a credit for his current cell phone usage.

As he was leaving my desk, he quipped, "Lunch is on me once I get the rebate check—oh, and you should write a book on how to do this."

It's funny how things work out.

So what are my qualifications for writing this book? I created annual reports for several years, and I dealt with the upper echelons of corporate management. I noticed that how quickly they responded to email if it were addressed properly and sent to the right managers. I also noticed that no employee wanted to have the CEO notice that the individual wasn't on his or her "A" game. So, when I had my first complaint with a large corporation, my first thought was to mail the head of the company to get results—and I did get results.

Ever since I filed that first complaint sixteen

years ago, I have emailed over seventy-five Fortune 500 companies using my method. I have received a response from upper management of the corporation within forty-eight hours. I get my problem fixed (and usually monetary rewards for my hassle) one hundred percent of the time. Yes, I know that's an incredible claim, but it's true.

Introduction

This book is about how to complain as a "little guy" to large corporations and get your problems solved via restitution or replacement by using a simple tool you probably use every day: email.

I'll go through the steps on how to get your email read and get results. Also included are examples of how problems with faulty services or merchandise were resolved through email. The companies I have emailed are some of the largest commercial entities in America. I've changed their names (for obvious legal reasons), but every email has produced positive results.

At the end of each chapter I've included key points to recap the chapter. These should be used to get you started quickly. However, it is recommended that you read the whole chapter and understand the full concepts explained first. Finally, I'll provide you actual emails I have written so that that you can use them as templates to get your own problem solved.

Let's see how my email method can get your problem in front of the decision-makers in the company and get the CEO to fix it!

Chapter 1
The Problem

Usually everyone I meet has a problem that has never been corrected. I've often heard: "Why should you complain? Nobody listens at these large companies. There is nothing I can do to get my problem corrected." The upper management of these companies loves this type of thinking. It saves them lots of money and even makes them money sometimes—if you buy another product of theirs to replace the one that is broken.

Unfortunately, the management of this company doesn't own the defective product or service. You paid for the service with which you are having problems. Or, you already own the product with which you are unhappy. So, you are stuck with it. The only recourse you have is to complain to get it fixed or replaced. This book deals with larger problems—some products you can take back to the store if you have the receipts. You could ignore the problems, but do you want to be reminded of them every time you look at the faulty product or use the erratic service?

Regardless, you have a right to make the company you purchased the item/service from aware of the problems you are having. Customer service and craftsmanship have virtually disappeared in the world today. Most companies have so many layers of management that they don't know these problems exist. You need to tell them what is going on down at the consumer level. This book will teach you how to reach up to the highest levels of these companies.

How do you reach into the upper echelons of these companies and get things fixed? One word: email. I know what you are thinking right now: "I throw away several hundred junk mail messages a day. A CEO isn't going to read my letter, let alone act on it." You are wrong. If you place the right wording in the subject line and follow certain guidelines that this book will teach you, the company you are petitioning will respond.

The reasons that you will get a response are pretty simple. First, almost all companies and all individuals within that company have email. This is a direct pipeline from the outside world that is relatively unfiltered. I am not condoning spamming people, but I support writing tactful and succinct emails that get results. All (good) CEOs read their email daily. This is their lifeline to the company.

Second, CEOs and executives have large egos, and they don't like to look bad in front of their peers and co-workers. If you make your problem known to more than one person that the CEO may see in an ordinary business day, they are compelled to solve the problem before they are questioned about it. Also, your email is a jolt to their ego. Most executives like to think their company is running on all cylinders and serving many happy consumers. Anything contrary to this is an eye-opening experience and is usually dealt with swiftly.

Third, bad news spreads. Everyone remembers a bad experience more prominently than several good experiences. A person may tell this experience to twenty people. Each one of those twenty people tells another twenty of their friends about your experience. Pretty soon you have hundreds of people talking about one bad experience. CEOs don't want this to happen.

Finally, people follow the path of least resistance. If something goes wrong with a purchase, most people buy a new item or don't shop at that store. Why do this? You need to take action and tell the leader of the company what is going on.

People need to take a stand and not take shoddy services and products for "the norm."

How do you know when you should take action? We'll look at that in the next chapter.

Chapter 2

Big Box Motor Corporation Complaint and Results Story

My first experience with the power of email was in the summer of 1992. I had just bought my first new car from Big Box Motor Corporation, and I was to start a new job the following week. So to celebrate I drove the car across the state to visit one of my friends and show it off for the weekend.

Ironically that Saturday, my friend and I were driving by the Big Box Motor Corporation dealership and suddenly the car lost power. We coasted into the dealer's lot. After celebrating our stroke of good fortune we went and found a mechanic who looked at my new, suddenly lifeless car.

It seems that my timing belt had frayed and broken, which caused the car to stop working. Since this was a weekend, they couldn't fit me in until Monday and I'd have to leave the car with them to work on it. Also, they didn't stock the part, so they would need to order the belt, which would further delay the repairs.

But I needed to be at my new job on Monday morning! We left the car at the Big Box Motor Corporation dealer, and I arranged to pick it up the following weekend. Luckily, we found a rental car company that was open, and I rented a car to get home.

The next weekend I returned, picked up my car, and the repairs were over $500. This was in addition to a six-day car rental bill. I was out about $700 on a brand new car. So, I decided to take action.

I emailed the CEO and the entire board of directors of the Big Box Motor Corporation. I explained to them that I was just out of school and bought a new car from their corporation and in the first week I was already being socked with $700 in bills to repair the vehicle and pay for a rental. I also sent them scans of the receipts.

A couple of weeks went by, but a response from the Big Box Motor Corporation did come in the mail. Their PR director wrote to me and apologized profusely for my misfortune. She wished me the best of luck in my new career and wanted my first car-buying experience to be a positive one, so she was enclosing a check for $700.

This experience made me a loyal Big Box Motor Corporation customer for fifteen years.

Chapter 3

Documenting the Problem

S o you have a defective product or service, and you want to get it corrected. The CEO or his management team will read your email, so you need to make sure you have done a few preliminary steps to make sure you have a convincing argument. Some may seem unnecessary, but you want to make sure you have a solid case.

The foundation of the letter to the CEO is based on the records you have kept since the transaction was completed, and what actions you have taken to get the product replaced or fixed.

You should keep records of the following:

    ✎ Initial receipts of the product or service.

    ✎ Phone calls made to customer service (your cell/landline phone bill is the best way to keep track of phone discussions since you can get the date, time and number of minutes you talked).

- ✐ Discussions with service personnel or technicians during on–site service calls.
- ✐ Discussions with clerks, managers or salespeople where you bought or ordered the product/service.

When you talk to any of these people, you should take notes. These should contain:

- ✐ The name and title of any customer service representative or managers.
- ✐ What was their attitude during the call? Remember, you are the customer. They should treat you with respect. If they are snippy, rude or condescending it makes your case stronger.
- ✐ If there was a recommendation of action, what was it?
- ✐ Did you feel they answered your questions correctly and knew about the product/service?
- ✐ What were the next steps going to be in solving your problem?

In these phone calls or face-to-face meetings, if anything is unclear, always ask, among other questions when a task will be completed. These questions may include when the new item will be delivered, what maintenance task has to be performed, and the status of an item on order. Leave nothing to chance. Otherwise you will probably end up calling them back and further prolonging the process. Also, remember your phone call is probably being recorded for "quality assurance."

Finally, keep documentation in a file on all monetary transactions and service calls for easy reference. Keep receipts, invoices, service call summaries, and special part orders (or experts who needed to look at your problem). It shows that you want the problem fixed and you are willing to take measures to get it done.

So if you have kept good records, you have your solid foundation to bring your case to the CEO. Also, you have all the answers to any questions he or she will have. Keeping your records organized will definitely help speed the process along.

Now that we have all the preliminaries complete, let's write that email.

Chapter 4

Big Box Phone Company Complaint and Results Story

I n the fall of 1999, I joined an Internet company and as one of their benefits they offered us a monthly reimbursement for a DSL service through Big Box Phone Company. I took them up on their offer, and the DSL was installed without any problems (or so I thought).

The service I had signed up for was a 1.2-megabit service. From their advertisements, my download speed should have been around 1.2 megabytes per second and my upload speed 256 kilobytes per second. Anytime I tried to use the service, my download speed crawled to around 56 kilobytes per second and my upload speed was even slower. For those of you that are of the non-technical persuasion, what this means is my Internet service was nowhere near the lightning fast speed that was advertised to me when I signed up.

Just to be sure I had done nothing wrong, I checked the connections around my house. Everything seemed to be fine. I ran speed tests online and verified the slow speed I was getting was not an illusion. I did troubleshooting tests with the manual on the router and on the computer. No luck. I wrote down all the data, and I called the customer service center for Big Box Phone Company.

When you call these customer service centers they usually run you through a "script." What this means is that they have a piece of paper for their customer service representatives to read to the customer that has a flow chart identifying common problems. I walked through this script with the first Big Box Phone Company customer service rep. This problem deviated from the script, and she didn't have any answers. She said a technician would come out to my house and test my line within two days. The results would be documented, and I could then call back and get those results.

I waited the two days and called the Big Box Phone Company back. The technician had checked my line and found no problems. Since this was a call center, I got a different representative. I asked for her supervisor. I spoke to him, and he ran through the same script again. He read me the same results from the technician and ran out of options. I asked for a more technically adept person, but he said he was the most senior on staff. He even tried to do some diagnostic testing to my router, but this was unsuccessful.

So, I decided to use my super slow connection and take action. I accessed the corporate information page on their Website to find the email addresses of the Big Box Phone Company's CEO, executive vice president in charge of their DSL program, and their PR department. I found not only the email addresses of all the members of the executive staff but their direct phone numbers! I typed up my email and sent it to their addresses and also left a very short but to the point voicemail. I also asked for a refund of the first three months of service.

I didn't have long to wait for a response. The very next day I was called at 9 am by a very frantic manager who appointed me my own case worker to make sure my system was up and running and to work with me to refund my money. The Big Box Company case worker was one of their lead technicians and knew exactly what was wrong after a few attempts at troubleshooting my router. He authorized a technician to come out to my house and fix the problem immediately.

The technician arrived, isolated the problem at my junction box, and fixed the problem in ten minutes. Later that day my email box contained a credit good for three months of online service.

Chapter 5
The Email

Your email will have a few special features that will get it noticed. Before you send it, you need to spell-check the email. Spelling and grammatical errors will undermine your case.

In your subject line, type: "Dissatisfied Customer Complaint." This is a way to make sure that your mail doesn't get dropped into all the junk mail the CEO probably receives every day. Also, you can flag your email as "Urgent" if you wish.

At the beginning of the letter in the upper left-hand corner, you need to include your full name, address, the date of the letter, and you also need to direct the letter to "Whom it may Concern." Do not address the mail to "Sir or Madam"—you don't know who will actually be reading the mail.

Your first paragraph should be very brief.

It should explain that you are a dissatisfied customer. It should also get to the point of why you are writing this letter. Explain in one to two sentences what your problem is. This is an introduction—you can go into more detail later. The last sentence should always express how disappointed you are with their company.

In the next two to three paragraphs, give a more detailed description and/or a timeline of the problem. Try to write only three to five sentences per paragraph. In these paragraphs you should be detailed but succinct. You should list any names of customer service people that you have been in contact with, the dates of company correspondence and what results you received, and if any additional fees have been assessed. All of these details should be pretty easy to summarize from your records. The last sentences in these paragraphs should always express how much time and money this process has taken—making and reiterating this point is important.

The next paragraph should reinforce how much money you have spent with their company in the past or during this transaction (if it's a substantial amount). If you have been a loyal customer for years, let them know. Also, if you have alternative options in your area (e.g., there is more than one hardware store in town), you can list those other vendors as alternatives to spending your money at their company.

The following paragraph should list your "requirements for resolution" in two points. Your first requirement should be that you want to get the item fixed or replaced. This should be stipulated that the repairs should occur at your convenience and on your schedule. The second requirement is a monetary amount based on the time you have spent trying to resolve the problem. Usually this will be a refund of the service or a credit for the item that is defective. Don't get greedy at this stage—you should have a logical amount in mind.

You then need to include how to get in touch with you. This may be your home or cell phone number. You should mention that the company should only contact you if they plan on resolving the issues you have listed in your demands.

The final item (besides your name on the bottom) is the date by which you want the company to contact you. Most companies will contact you within a day of receiving the email, but some have slower turnaround times. If a company doesn't respond, they do not have much regard for their customers.

Your email should be polite and to the point. Do not make accusations or waste words on anything that is not pertinent to fixing your problem. This is your opportunity to show you are businesslike and detail-oriented.

Read the email aloud to one other person. Ask the person to be objective about your email. Do they understand the problem? Is the wording too harsh? Are your demands adequate?

Chapter 6

Big Box Moving Company Complaint and Results Story

In the summer of 2003, my wife and I decided to move to Chicago. The company I was going to work for had an independent company relocate us. They commissioned Big Box Moving Company to take us from Minneapolis to Chicago.

I knew we were in trouble when the representative for the Big Box Moving Company came to our house and was supposed to bring some boxes, but he explained they wouldn't fit in his undersized sports car due to his golf clubs. He also did not bring any documentation to us except the basic corporate brochures. The more detailed "How to Move and Pack" brochures and "High Value Inventory" forms had to be requested via phone, and they didn't arrive until two weeks later.

We mentioned to the representative before he left that we needed as many boxes as he could give us, and he could bring it to the initial walkthrough. The next time he came to our house he brought us some boxes, but he said he couldn't fit any more in his trunk. While unloading his "packed" trunk (as he mentioned during our first meeting with him), the golf clubs still took up most of the space.

Upon reviewing the materials we called Big Box Moving Company with some standard questions, and it took several calls to get a decent answer. The process of exactly what would transpire with our inventory was still very vague until it was moving day.

The last few days before the move were very difficult. We confirmed two days prior to the move that the movers would be at our house the day before our house closed between 8 and 10 am. We also received a call one day before the move confirming the truck would be at our house at 8 am. We were called at 9:30 am and told that we would be called at 11:30 am with the new arrival time of the truck. No call came at 11:30. We called our customer service representative at Big Box Subsidiary (Big Box Company's local branch), and the representative had no idea of the situation that was unfolding. She asked us for information about who was driving the truck and other details she should have already had available. It took a call to our independent relocation representative to expedite the process. The truck didn't arrive until 3:45 pm.

The unloading of the truck occurred on time on the specified date in Chicago, but the movers in Chicago broke several items. These items (when inspected) were broken by careless packing of the truck, not by weak or inferior materials. The Minneapolis movers took their time and made sure everything was protected in the house, so they would not damage the woodwork in the house we were leaving. The Chicago movers were less careful and several walls of our new home were scratched and nicked. Also, we were told the items would be taken off the truck and checked off on our inventory worksheets. The unloading was so rapid that no chance was given to do this step. So, we had to go through our entire inventory in various rooms to make sure we received everything. To this day we are missing at least two boxes of various items that we were never able to locate.

We then filed a claim with Big Box Moving Company and sent in all the paperwork. We didn't get a response for several weeks. When we called customer service they said the items in question were not covered.

I acted by logging onto Big Box Moving

Company's Website and obtaining the identity of the CEO and the board of governance. I emailed them and waited for a response. The next day a representative called me about my problem (he was told by the CEO to "clear up this little matter"). He apologized for the misunderstanding and faxed me the claim forms as I was talking to him. He asked me the replacement costs for the damage and did not say anything about the claim not being eligible. I faxed him the information once I got off the phone. Afterwards, he called me back and we discussed getting reimbursed. This part went off without a hitch, and he told me I should receive my check in ten days.

We received the check ten days later, and we were able to replace everything that was broken.

Chapter 7

Sending the Email

You have an email ready to send. Now who to send it to? You need to find the email addresses of the people who make the decisions in the company. You do this by using their website. If you don't think the CEO's email is up there, you may be wrong.

First, you have to get not only the CEO's email but also the email addresses of the corporate governance committee and the PR director of the company. These are the people who are on the board of rectors and run the company.

Why do you want to send the email to all these people? They will probably apply pressure to the CEO to get the problem fixed. Also, the CEO can't sweep your matter under the rug. When more than one person knows of this problem, someone will be appointed to make your problem go away.

The PR director is an important element because they hate to see their company get bad PR and they end up wasting their time on complaints that could be easily fixed. Finally, people will try to save their own reputations by being proactive and fixing the problem before the CEO takes it up with them. Try to get at least six or more people from these lists.

So where do you find these addresses? They are on the company's corporate website. Find the main home page and look for the page marked "PR" or "Public Relations." You are looking for the press releases that have email addresses. It should be "someone@thecompany.com." Learn how the email address is formatted. For example it could be: jon.smith@thecompany.com, jonsmith@thecompany.com, or jsmith@thecompany.com.

Now, in the PR section should be the company's Corporate Governance section. This contains the names of the CEO and his or her management committee. You want the CEO's name and anyone you think would be responsible for the image of the company you are emailing. These people would have titles like "Brand Manager," "VP of Public Relations," and "EVP of Sales." Most publicly owned companies also have their financial documents online in their Investor Relations section (8K, 10K and 10Q are just a few examples), and within these documents are the top executives' names that sign off on the document. These are the people you should include in the email.

One hint about the CEO: He may use an alias or a nickname. You may have to read through some of the corporate literature to find out if he has a nickname. For example, a person may go by Bob@thecompany.com instead of Robert@thecompany.com. Include this variant in your email just in case.

Most of this information should be available on the Website, but if it isn't then you can order an annual report from the company to get the list of the corporate governance executives. Or you can go on popular financial websites like www.cbsmarketwatch.com to look at shareholders and other executives. This is probably your best bet since they pull from reliable financial sources. Also, Google is a powerful tool when trying to find out email addresses and names. A few quick searches through trial and error and you can locate almost anyone.

You can also call the companies and ask their secretaries for the CEO's email address, but this is pretty risky. Most secretaries won't give this information out.

Chapter 8

Big Box Department Store Complaint and Results Story

In November 2003, we decided to get new furniture for our living and dining room. We went and looked at all the chain stores, but we couldn't find what we wanted. So we decided to have our furniture custom made at Big Box Department Store. We placed our order, waited a few weeks for our furniture to be built, and were eager to have it delivered. However, we should have realized the delivery of our major purchase would not go smoothly.

We spent six Saturdays at home waiting for our undamaged furniture to arrive from Big Box Department Store. Furniture delivery is much like waiting for the cable guy (they give you a four-hour window that basically shoots your whole day). Each one of those Saturdays we sent back one or more pieces of furniture that were damaged. The console table we had ordered went back three times because of incorrect handling and loading by the employees (one time it was being rubbed on by another piece of furniture, another time it was dropped off the truck when they were unloading it, and the final time it was scratched by another piece of furniture that had dropped on it in transit).

After the third incident of receiving damaged pieces of furniture, we called our Big Box Department Store customer service representative to straighten out our order. After a week of leaving messages on the person's voicemail (her voicemail said she was on vacation), I called her supervisor. Her supervisor then told me that the person I was trying to reach had been fired. We also tried to contact the executive in charge of customer service, but they were also vacationing and too busy to return our calls (it turns out they were still employed after their vacation). After the next three deliveries of sub-par furniture, we decided to take action.

I logged onto the Internet, signed onto the Big Box Department Store corporate home page, found their corporate governance section and compiled a list of the CEO and the key individuals of the corporate governance board (one of them was the executive in charge of the entire chain). I composed an email asking them to deliver the undamaged furniture and reimburse me for the cost of one piece of furniture (the equivalent of my time spent at home those Saturdays), which was $698.

The following day the senior vice president in charge of Big Box Department Store's customer service called me. He was assigned to me by the CEO and the brand manager and was supposed to work with me to get my piece of furniture delivered on my terms and in pristine condition. He even planned to go to the warehouse and check it personally before it was loaded on the truck (which was little consolation since two times previously the piece was damaged on the truck). It arrived and was in perfect condition. I was ecstatic!

As mentioned previously I also asked for a reimbursement. I received a check in the mail from Big Box Department Store for $698 with a long letter of apology. We go to their store from time to time, but we only buy what we can see and take home with us. No more special orders!

Chapter 9
The Call

Most companies will respond to an email within 24–48 hours of receiving if it has been addressed to the CEO and his board. Usually the person who responds will be a manager or a personal case worker. The person has been instructed to correct your problem using any means necessary.

This experience with the company has probably been irritating, but you should be polite to the person who calls you. This individual has no idea what has transpired and is just getting up to speed on the situation. However, once you have been assigned a case worker, you are in control of the situation.

This person is someone you will be talking to quite extensively, so you will want to get his or her name and direct number or extension. You may also want to verify their title and position. You want to make sure the person has the authority to get your item fixed and get you compensated for your time. This person usually has authority, but it never hurts to be absolutely certain.

You will need to provide a synopsis of what has happened, whom you have talked to and what has been done so far. The records you have kept should make this pretty easy. You should also give the case worker a phone number where you can be contacted at any time. Finally, you should reiterate that you want your item fixed or replaced and to be compensated for your time.

Chapter 10

Big Box Hardware Store
Complaint and Results Story

In the fall of 2005 we decided to replace our kitchen, and one of the items we needed replaced was a back door to our deck. We used Big Box Hardware Store's "Big Box Lackey Service" to do the work. They were contracted to install an inner fiberglass door and an outer screen door with a hidden retractable screen. Due to sloppy workmanship and the inept structure of how Big Box Hardware Store supports the "Lackey Service," it took over ninety-four days to obtain parts to get the retractable screen for our screen door replaced and to repair the damage that was incurred during installation.

When the individual who worked for the contractor that Big Box Hardware Store commissioned installed the inner door, he damaged the weather stripping. We noted this to the installer. Also, a deadbolt that was purchased for the inner door was not installed correctly. Our locksmith noted this fact when he came out to redo the lock— he noted the strike plate and steel housing the deadbolt slides into was missing. We called the installer, and he came out the following week and fixed the parts. Since it was pleasant weather outside, we left the retractable screen down. When we tried to put the retractable screen up a week later, it did not work properly. We called the installer again and he came out and inspected the door.

The installer filed a damage report to Big Box Hardware Store's Lackey Service department, and I called to verify that the claim was made. The damage report was to tell Big Box Hardware Store that they might have to replace the door or get parts to fix it. Big Box Hardware Store explained it would take three weeks to get the part and they would then call us. I waited three weeks and called Big Box Hardware Store to find out the status of the part. The special orders rep at the Big Box Hardware Store where we purchased the doors said after researching our request that nothing had been done on it since the filing of the damage report three weeks prior. The rep was determined to prove that the individual store was not responsible for this oversight—the overlords of the Lackey Service department were the guilty party. This rep spent three weeks tracking down the problem and trying to find proof that this internal department was responsible for the delay. I had to make several phone calls per week to find out where we were in the process of getting the door fixed. I even had to take a phone call in the middle of a professional basketball game because the rep called me back at strange hours.

Four weeks after I initially called to find out the status, I found out the rep had faxed our request to our Lackey Service four times within the last three weeks. There was no response from this internal department. At this point, I finally took direct action. I called Big Box Hardware Store's Lackey Service and spoke to a supervisor at their call center. In the better interest of his job security, the supervisor would not give me his last name. After some research the supervisor called me back and mentioned how sorry he was that our order had not been acted on. He activated it and said he would give me a call the following week to tell me when the parts would arrive. He did not call, so I had to call him. It turns out the supervisor was too busy going to lunch but left word with the person I was calling to tell me the part was due in two weeks. By that date it would have been sixty-six days since my problem first started.

At that point I emailed Big Box Hardware

Store's president and the board of governors. The president was using his nickname to filter his email, but I had a suspicion of what it was because I read some of the press releases where he used his nickname.

In the email I made it clear that I am the customer. I wanted results, and I wanted them completed in an expeditious manner. I did not care who dropped the ball, who was to blame, or why the company needed to compile evidence to incriminate another party.

We also listed in our email the two things we wanted to have done. We wanted our door parts expedited and the damaged parts fixed to our satisfaction as quickly as possible. I also wanted the Big Box Hardware Store to follow up with me on a regular basis until this was completed.

Then I mentioned that I had spent hours on the phone trying to follow up where their system has broken down. Due to this incredible waste of our time I told them they should reimburse us the cost of the installation of the screen door and the entry door. The combined cost of these services was $375.

The following day I received a call from an individual in their Executive Support department. He was the person that would get our door fixed and authorize the cash for our troubles. I went over the details with him, and he said he would give me a status report in a couple of days. I hung up and got another call from the newly hired Director of Lackey Service. Again, I went over the details. Then the Regional Manager for the Lackey Service called, and I had to tell him the whole story again. This was just a verification of their inefficiency.

So the updates occurred, and they told me they would have a final status report for me the Friday after Thanksgiving. I asked the Executive Support rep if he was actually going to call me on that day. He assured me he would call with an update. When the day came, he never called—so I left a pretty harsh voicemail for him.

The next Monday the Executive Support rep called me, and he apologized profusely. He mentioned that he had spoken to the Regional Manager and had asked their company's "best man" to come out and look over the door that week. They would probably need to order parts, and once those parts had arrived I should call him back. Then they would send the workman out to fix my door. He also mentioned he would talk about compensation when the job was completed.

Later in the week the "best man" from the Lackey Service came out and assessed the door (while I was at work) and then the parts arrived the following week. I called the Executive Support department and told them, and the repairman came out the next day and fixed the door properly. He also noted several other mistakes in the original installation and fixed those as well. The final amount of time to get my door fixed? Eighty-nine days.

I called the Executive Support rep and told him the job was completed and I wanted to discuss compensation. By this time I had already paid off the credit card balance for the installation, so I wanted him to give me something other than a refund for the service. Since I am a homeowner and I do repairs frequently, I noted I could probably use a gift card to Big Box Hardware Store. He asked me the amount I would like and I said to double the cost of the door due to my time and effort, which would make the value of the card $750. He agreed and the card arrived in less than a week.

Chapter 11
Getting the Problem Fixed

Your primary goal is to get the item replaced or fixed. Make sure this happens by following up on the company's promises. This will probably require a few phone calls.

Before the item is delivered or a repair call is made, remember to address all the tasks that need to be completed. Explicit instructions are sometimes necessary to get all the requirements fulfilled. Do not assume that the person who will ultimately be responsible for overseeing the repair or replacement knows all the intimate details of your case. Sometimes a summary of your email is passed to your contact through word of mouth and they have not seen the actual email you sent.

If possible, try to get everything from the company in writing. This will provide you with a checklist of all the items necessary to complete your project. This list can be emailed or faxed to you. If anything is overlooked, you have evidence of what was requested and what was delivered.

It is always good to supervise the service call/replacement of the product. If you delegate this to another person they may not supervise up to your expectations, or the vendor may have questions only you could answer. In my case, several times a wrong part was delivered or it was damaged, so it was helpful to be there to point out the problems to the delivery/repairmen. If you have a checklist, this will help expedite things. Plus, it will probably be reported to the company's management who actually was there at the time the service was completed; so, your presence shows your commitment to getting your problem solved. Remember to note if there were problems with the attitudes of the company representatives or if you thought anything else was out of place (people were unprepared or late, you needed to provide them tools, etc.).

If the problem isn't solved with the service call/replacement, then you should call your contact at the company and let them know what happened. You are still the customer, and they should still try to make the situation right. At this point you'll probably need to schedule another service call or the delivery date of the replacement. Your company contact should realize that they would need to work around your schedule. Again, even though this is frustrating, you should be calm and polite as you work through the logistics of getting your problem solved.

Chapter 12

Big Box Appliance Company Complaint and Results Story

We moved into a newly constructed house and we needed to buy a new refrigerator, so we decided to buy one from Big Box Hardware Store since they matched our best price and could deliver it within a few days.

This story had a few more players than most of our other complaint emails. The first player was Big Box Hardware Store, where we paid up front, and they issued us a purchase order and a receipt. The second was Big Box Appliance Company, which provided the refrigerator based on the purchase order, and the last was Local Delivery Service, which was contracted by the Big Box Hardware Store to deliver the refrigerator to our house.

We ordered the refrigerator on a Monday in the beginning of November and were told that it would be delivered on Saturday. Remember that our house was new construction, and we would not have a refrigerator until one was delivered. Luckily, my wife was traveling that week and I was working overtime, so not having a refrigerator for a few days didn't make much difference. As long as we had one by Thanksgiving, it would be fine.

That Saturday I received a call from Local Delivery Service, and they told me that they could not deliver the refrigerator since it had arrived damaged from Big Box Appliance Company. They said they would be reordering the appliance and I would be called by the Tuesday of next week with a new arrival date.

I waited until Wednesday and called the Local Delivery Service and they received no word from Big Box Appliance Company of when they were going to deliver it. I called them back on Friday and still received no answer; so, I called Big Box Appliance Company customer service. I talked to a very genial customer service representative who said she could look up my order from my home phone number. She said it would be at Local Delivery Service's warehouse in a couple of days.

So I called Local Delivery Service at the end of the business day to tell them that the refrigerator was supposed to be delivered, but they had not received any refrigerator. So the next day I called the Big Box Appliance Company support line again and asked to speak to a manager. He informed me that he needed a Big Box Appliance Company Purchase Order Number or he could not help me with the request. This is not on Big Box Hardware Store's invoice sheet, so after work I had to go to Big Box Hardware Store and get this number. The service desk manager found it and called Big Box Appliance Company's support line. We waited for over an hour while they tried to locate our refrigerator in their systems and warehouse.

From what I can tell by the discussion with the customer service representative, once a damaged appliance is returned to Big Box Appliance Company, it almost vanishes from their computer system because it is manually replaced. So, she could not locate it until she had someone physically verify where the appliance was. Big Box Appliance Company sells millions of dollars' worth of refrigerators per year, and they do not track these in their inventory via computer? That was difficult to believe.

So I emailed Big Box Hardware Store and told them of my trouble. The manager of the local Big Box Hardware Store was assigned to me as my case worker, but he was unable to help since Big Box Appliance Company was the actual supplier of the refrigerator. He did help encourage Big Box Hardware Store to apply pressure to Big Box

Appliance Company to solve the problem.

After the Big Box Appliance Company customer service rep located our refrigerator, we were told it would be delivered on the Friday after Thanksgiving. The refrigerator was delivered, and as we were about to hook up the water line we noticed a large gash across the back of the refrigerator—like someone had swiped it with a forklift. The damage on the back was quite substantial. Whatever had hit it had put a dent in the back about four inches long, snapped the water lines, and gouged the whole back of the appliance. To top it all off, we inspected the packing boxes for any indication that this refrigerator would have been damaged and the boxes were undamaged. So, someone at Big Box Appliance Company had packaged this already damaged refrigerator up and shipped it off.

I called Big Box Appliance Company's customer service line and spoke to the manager I talked to previously. I was first offered a $50 certificate for any new Big Box appliance. I laughed and told him I wanted to be reimbursed for my time, inconvenience, and inept delivery on Big Box Appliance Company's part. The rep then offered me a check of $75. I turned him down.

So I emailed the Big Box Appliance Company and included the CEO, marketing director and the president of Big Box Appliance Company's consumer division. The next day I was emailed by the president of the consumer division and told that someone would be contacting me shortly.

The following day I received a call from the executive assistant to the president of the consumer division at Big Box Appliance Company. I told him my problem. He said that a new refrigerator was on the way, and I told him I expected to be reimbursed for my time and trouble, which I thought was equal to the cost of the refrigerator. He balked at that and then wisely said we should wait until my refrigerator was delivered to talk about compensation.

The new refrigerator arrived the following weekend, and it was in perfect condition. The men from Local Delivery Service were told that they were to do "whatever it takes" to make me happy.

The next week I called the executive assistant back at Big Box Appliance Company and told him the refrigerator had been delivered. He said that he was willing to offer me a complimentary warrantee along with my $75 check. I laughed and told him I had already purchased the unit with the warrantee. So, I told him that I would take $250 in cash, which was significantly lower than the cost of the refrigerator. He agreed, and my check arrived the following week.

Chapter 13

Compensation

Once the repair or replacement is complete, then you can ask for compensation. Usually the amount of compensation is dependent on several different aspects. One of these is the willingness of the company to make sure you are a satisfied customer. If the company wants to make amends then the amount of concessions they are willing to make will be higher. If they are begrudgingly trying to make the problem go away, your compensation will probably be minimal.

Remember that the company's attitude works both ways—if the company has been helpful, then you should take that into account. If the company has been difficult, then you should try to get as much as you can for your time and effort. Use your best judgment—you want to start out with a reasonable amount and not make extraordinary demands.

Another determining factor of the amount of compensation is how good of a negotiator you are. Unless you know exactly the amount you want, you should always let the company name the first figure. One of the most common phrases in negotiation is, "Is that the best you can do?" After an the initial offer and every counteroffer, if you say that one phrase the company will probably continue to sweeten the reward until they reach the maximum amount they are willing to give.

Cash isn't the only compensation that companies can give. Gift cards, free warrantees, and extended service contracts can also be a part of your reward. So, even if the company turns down your cash reward there are other avenues you can explore. Gift cards are a minimal expense to the company and are probably the easiest form of compensation for a company to distribute. Company checks require approval, so the time you will be waiting for your reward will be longer.

Chapter 14

Big Box Gyms Complaint and Results Story

I had been a member of Big Box Gyms for six years, and my wife fifteen. We both had what we thought was the highest membership level. One day, several guys I worked with went to a newer, larger installation of this gym company, and I decided to join them.

I expected to have no problems with walking in, submitting my membership card and working out. However, this particular club was a "Bigger" Big Box Gym and required an additional fee. They allowed me to work out that day on a trial basis. I looked around and thought that the amenities they had there were no different than the ones I had at the gym I usually went to near our home.

When I got home, I called Big Box Gyms' customer service and spoke to a rep. She informed me that the individual gym enforces these extra fees and that there was nothing she could do. I explained to her that she was misinformed—Big Box Gym is the parent company, so the home office would have influence over their pricing. The representative made no effort to make any sort of compromise.

After this discussion I wrote the CEO of Big Box Gyms and told him I was very displeased that I needed to pay additional fees on top of what we already were paying to use this particular gym. I explained that the name variant was nothing but a marketing gimmick and the only thing that they accomplished was alienating a member of their gym. I also told him we did not want to pay the extra dues to use this particular location, and we have started to take actions to terminate our membership with Big Box Gyms and join another gym where we can use all their facilities for one rate.

The following day I received a call from the CEO's personal assistant—the CEO had read my email, and the assistant wanted to negotiate with me on the CEO's behalf to keep my membership. I explained to him that I wanted to use these clubs at the base rate that my wife and I were already at. In between his responses I could hear him typing on a computer or doing figures on a calculator. He gave me a couple options that were definitely lower, but not at the rate I was willing to pay to use the club.

However, I wanted to run the figures by my wife to see if she thought any of these rates would work for us—one of them cut our health club fees by over 50%! I asked if I could call him back tomorrow with a verdict. After some discussion with my wife she mentioned that she wanted to change to a different club anyway, so I called them back and turned down Big Box Gyms' best offer.

Even though we didn't take their best offer, this story proves that the CEO did read the mail, had a case worker call us, and we could have saved substantial money on our memberships. This, all from one email!

Chapter 15
Complaint Not Addressed

Once the people who you have complained to receive your email, you want someone to call you and work with you to make sure that your problem is being fixed. However, everything does not go as planned. You may get an adverse response or no response at all. If you do not hear from the company for at least two weeks (people do go on vacation) or if you get an adverse response, you may have to take stronger measures.

The first is to phone the CEO or speak to members on the governance committee. If a secretary turns you away, ask for the person's voicemail. If you leave a voicemail for each person, they will see that you will not go away easily. Again, do not be rude—you want them to help you get your problem fixed.

You can also write another email reiterating your problem and stress to them that you will be spreading the word about your problem to whoever will listen—friends, co-workers and even the media. Newspapers and TV news usually has a soft spot for the underdog in these "David versus Goliath" stories. Companies know this and will try to avoid this negative publicity (this is where sending an email to the PR Director will help you).

The email can also mention that their unwillingness to resolve the issue brings into question the integrity of their company. This can also be useful in getting a response. This implies the CEO and his governance committee will lose face. As mentioned in previous chapters, most CEOs are very sensitive to this perception.

You can also write that you will be informing the Better Business Bureau in their area that your complaint has not been addressed. This is a lengthy process and should be used sparingly.

If the company does reply but their response isn't what you expected, you should try to negotiate with them to reach an agreement. It is possible that the compensation you are requesting is too high or the wording of your email may be offensive. Remember, you want them to help you get your item repaired or replaced. You must keep this in mind if their response is less than adequate.

Finally, make sure the person addressing the problem can give you results. It may have been forwarded to someone in a position who cannot give you the resolution you seek. So, if this is the case, work with this person to give you another contact—one who can help you resolve the problem quickly and who has the authority to give you what you want.

Chapter 16
Actual Complaint Emails

To help you write your emails, I wanted to include a couple of my emails that were sent to the companies mentioned in the preceding chapters.

⌘   ⌘   ⌘

Actual email to Big Box Department Store about our damaged furniture:

To Whom It May Concern:

You are receiving this email because I am a very dissatisfied customer, and I have waited for results from your employees regarding my furniture purchase from Big Box Department Store.

We ordered our furniture in November 2003 and have sat home six Saturdays waiting for undamaged furniture to arrive. However, we have sent back several pieces of furniture that were damaged. One piece has gone back three times because of the incorrect handling and loading onto the truck by your employees.

We spent over $7,000 on our purchase, and we are so outraged by the lack of customer service that we will never purchase anything from your store again. We have tried to resolve this by calling Mrs. X, but she was much too busy vacationing to answer our requests.

What we want from you are two things:

- We want the piece of furniture we ordered delivered in a timely manner without any defects. We will specify when we will have it delivered.

- We have wasted enough time waiting for the correct merchandise you seem to be unable to deliver. Due to this incredible waste of our time we believe you should reimburse us the cost of the final piece of furniture. This piece of furniture cost $698. We have already paid off our bill in full, so we would like a check in this amount as a gesture of goodwill.

If you wish to resolve the above issue, you may contact me at home at 555-1212 or on my cell at 555-1212. Only contact me if you plan to fulfill the points listed above.

If I do not get a satisfactory response by July 8, I will be forced to use other means to make my point.

Regards,
Christopher Mielke

⌘　⌘　⌘

Actual email to Big Box Gyms about their membership fees at different clubs:

To Whom It May Concern:

You are receiving this mail because I am a very dissatisfied customer. I have been a Big Box Gym member for six years. My wife has been a member of Big Box Gym for fifteen years.

Apparently the amount we pay for our Deluxe memberships is not enough for your exclusive clubs. The clubs I am speaking of are your Big Box Gym Super Clubs. I went to the Big Box Gym Super Club in the north side of Some Town, Illinois, and was informed by the staff that I had to pay extra dues (a Deluxe Plus membership) to use the club. This is outrageous. This Super Club is no different than the clubs in My Town, Illinois. The Big Box Gym Super Club allowed me to work out for one day.

This name change is nothing but a

marketing gimmick and the only thing you have accomplished is alienating two of your members.

We are not paying extra dues to use this particular location, and we have started to take action to terminate our membership with Big Box Gyms and to join another club where we can use all their facilities at one rate.

I called your customer service and spoke to Mrs. X. She informed me that the particular club enforces these extra fees, and there was nothing she could do. I believe she is misinformed—Big Box Gyms is the parent company, so you have influence over their pricing. Your customer service representatives should do everything in their power to ensure that their members are satisfied with their membership. She made no effort to make any sort of compromise.

If you waive the extra fees to use this facility, we would be happy to stay with Big Box Gyms.

You may contact me at work regarding this matter at 555-1212 or on my cell at 555-1212. If I do not get a response from you by August 31 we will look at other options for our workouts.

Sincerely,
Chris Mielke

Chapter 17
Conclusion

I hope this book will help you get results with any problem you need to have fixed. Even though this method seems very simple and straightforward, this streamlined method will help you get a response from any company in very short amount of time.

About the Author

Chris Mielke lives in Holly Springs, North Carolina, with his wife and calculates he has written over 1.3 million emails by the time this book was published. Thankfully, less than 1,000 were complaint emails.

www.ingramcontent.com/pod-product-compliance
Lightning Source LLC
Chambersburg PA
CBHW060641290526
45793CB00001B/341